Also by Marina Brown

LAND WITHOUT MIRRORS

LISBETH

WALKING ALONE TOGETHER

AIRPORT SKETCHES

THE LEAF DOES NOT BELIEVE
IT WILL FALL

Poems

by

Marina Brown

Gilberte Publishing
Tallahassee

Published by:

Gilberte Publishing
5377 Paddington Drive
Tallahassee, FL 32309

Printed in the United States of America

Design by Marina Brown and Douglas Kiliman

The Leaf Does Not Believe It Will Fall / by Marina Brown
1. Poetry – Collections

ISBN 978-0-9897543-1-6

First Edition

In thanks for

the people, the places, the great loves,

the profound losses, and the precious moments

that are made explicable by poetry.

Contents

The Seasons' Turns

Visits with the Muse

Traveling in Time

A Place of Solace

Puycelsi, France

THE LEAF DOES NOT BELIEVE
IT WILL FALL

THE SEASONS' TURNS

Spring's Morning

Patent-leather body in a yellow fur wrap

Trampolining in flower-arcs on the budded bush.

Azalea-ravishing acrobat,

Who do you think you are

Harrier-jetting cursive fugues in this fine spring air?

Little Lazarus mounds, rolled in heaps,

A winter's battleground, a marble-field of death,

Still acorn-capped and dirty, only heads left to roll

Till spring rain turns corpses

To a thousand soldier sprouts.

I want a bee to land on my hand,

for us both to feel unafraid.

I want to watch a mosquito ride its raindrop from a cloud.

I want the squirrel to love me and lay an acorn at my feet.

I want my soul awakened from its deepening sleep.

Spring's Afternoon

Where does smoke come from on this translucent day

With no fire or fog or haze to hamper the clouds at play?

Where does smoke come from when winter's hearths are

scraped and washed and oak logs dutifully covered in

green plastic tarp?

As elusive as sadness that floats among the trees

Pierced by the clatter of the desiccated leaf,

Smoke is a chocolate swirl made from empty air

                    And leafy hopes,

                    And dreams all spent

                    That tangle my hair.

April at Lake Overstreet

He didn't see me...

the old man staring at the water

under the thick wrists and drooping fingers of the oak.

The sun hit his sagging jowl beneath a faded cap,

while with cocked head he appraised the distant shore,

fixed the reeds with curiosity,

and listened to the tits and clicks of frogs

and silhouetted birds.

He might have been St. Francis

as a squirrel dared a nearby nut

and a beetle settled languidly on his leg.

Even Spanish moss circled toward him

swooning into furry halo his silhouette.

Or perhaps he was Seurat, for about him solids dissolved

into daubs of light,

chartreuse and ruby, opaline blues, bounding titanium

pools that throbbed like heart beats

when the wind blew and when the old man

moved his arm against the sun.

Or he might have been God—this man—this tired farmer

surveying a watery acre he had made, fertilized and fed

until beauty spilled from lake and brush with twirling fish

and acrobatic bugs

        to please their Father's gaze.

Then gravel rolled beneath the feet that clattered along

the path,

Shouts and whoops dislodged the air. A puppy took a slap.

Interlopers don't dream in color nor count the hairs of

                                bees,

Nor trace a silver ripple as it dilates into death.

Nor notice an old man's silence or ages passing by,

        nor how quickly fall the insects

        against a hissing spray.

How Shall I Call Thee?

A Mogul's palace?

A tiered pink extravagance on the verge of the

 insufferable?

The over-arching chutzpah of a spoiled child's house of

dolls?

A pink chandelier of a thousand blooms that attracts even

as its sexual come-ons scatter in greasy petals on the

dried, brown straw?

A tulip tree, a whore in damsel's clothes.

A burlesque show, without the songs.

And with my own Two-Lips, oh, histrionic tree,

I blow you a kiss-off.

The Good Morning

Conversations everywhere.
"Breakfast!"
     "This branch is taken."
"You're handsome."
     "Mama, I'm hungry!"
"I'll build you a nest."
     "I'll give you babies."

In the Chesapeake's villages, slumbering close by the
memory tracks laid down by plantation owners, fishermen
and old rebels,
There is only silence.
Too early yet for the oystermen and crabbers whose
burnished skin will soon reflect the pink of dawn.
Only avian conversations for now, arranging the day.

Ghostly herds of milk cows parade the rolling pastures,
Munching wraiths who stroll to cricket's tunes.
A squadron of geese on their way to Africa seem asleep on
the morning air,
Primordial wings like black crucifixes stretched against a
salmon sky.

And slowly, the contours of day fill in.
Deep green outlines on a chartreuse lawn,
Purple shadows reflecting red.

A shore bird emerges from a curtain of reeds,
a diva expecting applause.
But only a gull astride a fish—now on its way to heaven—
bothers to lift its head
And cackle a morning salutation.

Summer's End

Ahead, spangled in chocolate daubs, caramel streaks, and
vanilla's bawdy dashes,
A painted forest hides itself
In leaves and vines of khaki,
Moss of camouflage green.

A heartbeat in a puddle, a spider's elegant strut,
Mosquitoes riding raindrops upside down.
The woods will not be quiet, its colors up in arms,
While tendrils shout at sunshine from below the dirt's dark
smudge.

The grove masquerades in shadow,
Disappeared into itself,
When single trees, like naked elves, emerge to flaunt their
charm.
A cloudy pass, the wind's relapse,
Interrupts their strip-tease,
Then daunted, shy and chastened, they seek their former
weave,
In a lace of green embroidery, sylvan dances stilled.

Now as I stop, around me, a chanted song begins,
Insects sing the lines the trees still yearn to whisper.
Here they know the plot, played ten thousand years,
A circular thought, replayed, remade—no need now for
sequelae.

And if, they say, when death arrives, you exit without
suffering,
Your eternity too, will be so blessed,
No expunging nor erasing ...
Then let me die with a poem begun,
Its words formed on my lips,
And let me drop, like the leaf that falls ...

Hovering, lingering,
              gently eddying on such August air.

On Little Dead Children

I stop for a moment to listen to what I cannot see—
to imagine calligraphy scrawled overhead,
And in the wind, as it coils and worries and blasphemes
this afternoon,
I sense another's stir—a cadre's fearful shift.

A scratching. Of feet? Or fingers or claws?
Refugees tossed from their beds?
Or terrified children who must flee from the shots?
Angels that fly from the carnage?

The bullet-shaped leaves, corpses as seen from the air,
are fingered and stroked—necromancing wind—
 yet now lay strategically still.
Then a moment, a chance, a hatch, an escape,
a sheet tossed over the wall.

The dead come alive, on the run, in a sprint, zombies not
knowing they're lifeless.
And I continue my walk, the wind in my hair, supplicant
leaves at my ankles,
Ignoring their caws, the rasps of their curses,

Ignoring the passing of seasons.

February

The trees are dreaming

I see their warm winter sighs lying across the forest as they breathe.

And if I am still,

If the bird doesn't wake,

And the firefly sleeps,

I'll go dreaming too.

A steady pine,

Eyes closed tight,

Anonymous and free

Dressed in a gown of whispers.

March Impressions at Maclay Park

Alligator ripples,
Or just the wind?
Or inspiration—
In-coming like a bomb.

The oak's trunk flowing
Like lava in crusty fjords
captures my fingers along with other's lives in its leafy
Vesuvius.

He waits in the rigging,
Little turquoise acrobat, suit pulled tight—
Shaking in the wind, a shimmy for a gnat
That somersaults by in the breeze.

The patent-leather leaves of the magnolia
Clattered and fought—
A rain-shower on a metal roof,
Angry, leafy harridans on this sunny day.

This vista—a charcoal sketch,
Its shadows inky and undulating,
Smudged a soft pastel by the wind,
Where the Spanish moss pretends to be an anemone,
Fingers rippling in a substance neither liquid nor vapor.

The Journey

"Like a log. You've got to stick your arms up over your head and roll!"

I rotate down the hill, hip bones meeting rocks and bosom-crushing roots. Head jerking, the tall grass appears and disappears again and again before my eyes.

Vermont is still filled with fragrance, even this late in autumn. And having completed my revolutions, I now lay submerged in sweet brindle grass and wrinkled yellow leaves, gulping lungsful of strange moribund pheromones from the summer's end.

Soon we would all traipse back to the stone house that somebody's uncle had risked us for the weekend. We would pick apples and peel and boil them. Some we would cover in cinnamon and sugar and bake into pies. And some we would throw like children or chew like well-favored horses who'd chosen that day not to buck.

The sky would have dripped cerulean fingers along the globe of the sky—if there were such a thing that day. But it stayed in its place. And the earth and the plants did the same. Recalcitrant apples bobbed and tugged at their stems and eventually, in some misguided belief in independence, broke free to plummet in tiny scalloped arcs down the hill.

And why not make the break? Is a pie so much better? No, better to lie amid the stalks and brush, feeling your substance relax into soil, knowing your final fragrance will pleasure a faraway deer—and to know such things as a higher calling.

And so, I push off, resuming my roll, arms reaching up, legs stretched behind, over and over and over until—on another autumn day, under an azure sky,
> a deer will lift its head in the forest
>> and move its nose to the wind.

Upon a Midnight Clear—a Christmas Story

It hadn't helped that it had started to rain—or maybe it was snow by now. On the back of the motorcycle, her helmet was pelted with specks of something wet and cold.

Ten hours and 700 miles earlier it hadn't been much different—only drier.

"Who do you think you are? A couple of players? Gett'n it all for free?" the manager had yelled when they couldn't pay. "I'm runnin' a motel, not a shelter. Now get the hell out!" And he'd slung their backpacks and a tiny cooler out toward the dumpster.

For the next several hours they'd settled themselves into the warmth of the big metal garbage can, finding a blessed package of dinner rolls and an old hoodie that incongruously read, "Virgin Airlines." But then the rain had started and the organic parts of their dumpster mattress had begun to sag, and they'd decided it was better to just be on the road.

He'd told her that by the time they hit the desert, the weather would clear up. He'd made it sound like Arizona was one big dune, ruddy in the sunshine and warm to the touch. She'd even pictured herself rolling down the big hips of piled sand, maybe building a sandy version of a snowman or stripping down to her underwear to get a tan. But as wetness seeped into the folds of her hoodie, she remembered what a liar he was. Always had been.

There was the "I've got a good trade" speech, the one where he'd lorded it over the bartenders who stood vacant-eyed in the fragrance of the afternoon's stale beer. "Yeah, I coulda' been a cop. I coulda' been in airconditionin'. But I got a trade that I can take anywhere and make a buck—a good buck. I'm a journeyman carpenter and don't nobody who can take that away." Of course, most of it was a lie. He'd pounded a few nails onto a few roofs—and for the rest of it—well, at forty, cleaning tables in a roadside bar wasn't much of a profession.

But when you're pretty, sixteen, and on the prowl, and nobody much cares about your ID, a good-looking guy with a smooth line, some swagger and a vintage 'hog' looks pretty good.

Hmmm… Good thing nobody had ever looked real hard at that ID, she smiled to herself. She had a famous last name, for God's sake. Related down through the years to some high muckety-muck. It'd never mattered to her. That long-ago rich guy was history and as far as she was concerned, only good for getting out of a speeding ticket—if she were lucky.

Right now, all she wanted was a place to lie down. The wet snow had stopped and on the back of the bike it was suddenly brutally cold. Overhead, the desert sky extruded one pinpoint star that as it rose, grew oddly larger in the lonely blackness.

She put her hand inside the leather jacket he had given her when she first climbed on his bike, and inside the flannel of the Virgin jacket from the dumpster. Even now, nine months after they'd met, and eight months after she'd known, the perfect dome of her belly still surprised her when she touched it. Yeah, it was funny—he'd always told her it was safe, something about a vasectomy. But, oh well, what was done, was done. She'd known he was a liar and it was probably her own fault.

But the baby was something else. Hard to think about it. But she would be a good mother—better than the one she'd had. And she would raise this baby to be special. Maybe, she thought... maybe even someone who would change the wor...

And then the front wheel of the bike hit the ice and the star began to spiral, and after the crash, tiny pieces of chrome still floated in the night air, clattering to the desert floor, like so many fragments of the firmament of Heaven.

And there was quiet upon the land,

      except for the lowing of a cow

        which seemed to weep in the darkness.

Again, Spring

Through the fog
That turns trees to aquarelles,
Feathered divas in contrapuntal choir
Hand off arias and daring solos in interlocking fugues.
They play out Rigoletto and mourn Bohème
                    —even before the sun can shine.

And at my feet, layers of unraked leaves shift like a crusty
ocean,
Quietly devouring themselves in the spring's warmth and
wet,
Unconcerned in their slow transmogrification
        by azaleas' boisterous fuchsia,
                    Or the nodding white heads of lilies.

Black as iron against a pewter sky, the mockingbird plumps
his silhouette,
Master of his universe, he wisely disappears
with the turn of my head or a finger's random lift,
in a transient's epiphany that his season is but short.

VISITS with the MUSE

The Sleeping Muse

As I rise, my muse lies sleeping in sepia.

With a metaphor's pillow and a simile's drape,

She slumbers in night ink, preparing for her entry into the

pattern of the egg's crack, and the smell of leather gloves,

 the ripples of wood grain, the silent cricket who watches

in the dark.

Would I rouse her if I mold my form to hers and fold a leg

and kiss her neck and stroke her breast and steal at the

little butterflies that dance in garlands above her head

the words that flow in exhalation?

Should I try?

A Flower's Waltz

With their intake of air,
the exhalation that didn't come,
They knew something miraculous had happened.
They had seen the leap, a grand jeté,
the earthly bird overcoming gravity,

Toes pointed, back arced,
the bow stretched before release.
In the moment between the music's throb and beat,
In the space between flight and earth
I'd slipped from my body, no longer constrained,
And flowed into each of theirs—both of us made of water.

Into each seat and heart,
The curtain, the stage,
proscenium's gold and dark,
All molecules blended; I'd read their thoughts,
And become Buddha and the Christ,

Then, with the next note's ring, I landed my leap
as the music sang its song.
Suspended breath was breathed again,
the planets turned an inch,
A thousand years away, I'd spent, on a trip to visit God,
A stardust dance, a heartbeat's pause,
a slip across the Curtain.

The Poet's Morning

The word,

The phrase,

The ribbon of analogy,

The secret in the shadow,

The metaphor grazed, its filament touched,

And lovely similes spied.

So near... so near... and then...

The coffeepot's lid finds the counter.

Fresh beans, by god, must be ground.

Knives and spoons and ceramic plates and the gasket's

suck and the stove top's iron

In conspiratorial pleasure

Hammer, slam and beat each other,

Knock and tremble, groan and clang

Their arrhythmic chaos of superficial glee—

Perverse morning sounds that snatch my dream-time's

masterpiece,

And clip, clip, clip my web, my spider's silk of words.

The Conductor

He told me he sees dancers

In the moments when his eyes are closed,

Or when his gaze peers through darkness at a hundred

beating hearts.

He told me he sees ribbons,

Innuendos in rhythmic waltz,

Teasing for a minuet, a gambol or gavotte,

Bending him in sarabandes—set free before the crowd.

He didn't tell me more. Nor did I ask about inspiration,

Or how loneliness feels

      when the pretty dancers leave.

Enough to see his spirit lift—a German mist in spring,

To watch him dance with spinners,

      Or leap in Slavic maize.

He didn't have to tell me

that in starlight in a forest

      He becomes the satyr about to mount the nymph.

On My Art Exhibition Being Taken Down

They were unsure in the beginning,

Reticents, not knowing where to stand,

what posture to take,

As if they'd been asked to pose with teacups

on farm-blistered fingers, as if the columns and mullions,

the vaults and glistening floors would heighten

the gauche calamity of their best clothes.

The evangelist had bridled that with Bible held high,

nobody watching would whisper the name of Jesus.

And the old man cleaning fish—a puny catch of blue gills

not fit to feed his young—

stared back at his watchers, an aquarelle fist swelling its veins,

His grandson, armed with a curse.

But in the long afternoons of April and May,

as light squares cubed the floor Mondrian-style,

These dark people settled in.

Settled, as nomads always do,

Making this place their own, climbing its walls in vibrant

Exultation, swinging their breasts, hoisting their haunches

From church pews and beer-scented dives.

They looked at each other,

lonely men and elegant whores,

Women singing in churches and dancing at graves,

While a Santarian chant soothed a dead man's soul,

And outside, motorcycles flayed the air like flesh.

These maids and slaves and dancers and pray-ers

And dried-up and fat and dying and dead

Have made a home here.

No longer shy, they shimmy in a master's house,

And find they love the stares of admiring strangers who for

once seem to see.

A shaggy-haired girl asks if she can stay.

"A closet? A corner?"

Here in the solace of stillness that comes when the

caretaker leaves.

The old man beside the fireplace gazes in eternal
resignation,
And others cry out in hymns to God, begging to be left to
sing from these walls,
In this manila light, their stories on watercolor lips.

But like a mother abandoned, I must take them with me.
I am pregnant again, and pregnant with others again
tomorrow.
For these—these gestated utterances of my brush and my
heart—this was their moment, their reunion, their zenith,
brothers and sisters dancing at the ball.

But midnight has struck, the car is running,
And my children must leave for home.
Come home to their cupboards, to the empty house,
To the darkened bedroom,
where they will imagine themselves praised once again.

TRAVELING in TIME

The Skyscrapers of Hong Kong Harbor

Hong Kong diamonds, stacked in cubes,

Parade their charms like statuesque whores,

As watery minions dash to Kowloon's feet,

licking at their old perfume.

By night, their throats thrown back

and stretched in sparkling strut,

one might mistake them for tipsy odalisques.

But drifting through forests of concrete cells,

A sickly innuendo of the future

circles this harem like a snake.

Passionless courtesans, drenched in sweat,

Dance when there is no music.

Hong Kong's pillars made of diamonds sparkle—

Just as zircons always do.

Amazon, Amazonia

Like a tangible respiration, the Amazon hovers above itself
Watching its image born again in morning light.

Woven in and out of jungle green,
the fog vaporizes in the early heat
As gifts of madeira, bananas,
and in flood times, a chicken fearfully traveling alone—
continue their liquid pilgrimage from Andean heights.

Canoes, long and severed from the jungle,
stick pointy wooden noses in the air and slither, like
determined snakes, quietly borne down by the family
inside.
Bundling together, dugout deep, their brown faces thick
from sun and water,
They watch the watchers in the jungle's weave,
acknowledging each call of bird, shift of sloth, the
monkeys' lacey silhouettes,
Or the roll of a dolphin, as pink as lips freshly kissed

The Amazon carries them and sometimes villages too
(muddy banks nothing to be counted on.)
A house walks on heron legs, hiding from the water,
yet sprawled open to welcome the night and the day and
the cool breezes that circle its hammocks' arc.
It sits among its neighbors—an innocent playground for
parrots and parents and children
who tumble in troops and mimic their elders until they too
are old.

The vein and artery, the pulsing heart of Amazonia,
the river circles itself like a mighty ringlet around a
landscape of trees that force themselves, through sheer
will, to rise from a thin and shifting soil.

And the forest's handmaidens, black-winged vultures,
Kiskadee, and hawks who primp like movie stars,
lift high, then drop, the semen of the jungle,
a future promise that Paradise may not be lost.

And now they come—footsteps pushing aside the mist,
treading near a slumbering snake, a fidgety frog, or the
walking bones of a dog.
The village shoulders child and sack, dry thatch, or—with
luck—the silvery flash of a fish,
still wiggling it's worth to market.

At water's edge children play or invisibly squat,
become blades of grass or clots of mud,
and just as brown, and sweetly malleable, they hurl their
bodies high, abandoning themselves to the air and the
chocolate river.

And pretty girls too, in colors and beads, their new breasts
beckoning toward motherhood's lure,
Cluster and giggle at boatmen's stares, then wrapping
their catch in a fresh green leaf,
hurry home for its eating.

Amazon, Amazonia, a delicate world,
Clasped in brown fingers but desired by the rest,

Amazon, Amazonia, your petals and stems,
Arboreal armor and watery shield,

You mother, you mumble,
And rage and recede,
And feed us and curse us, and move toward the sea.

Forgotten brown children grow strong in your glades,

A jaguar lies alone in the forest.

A cell phone is ringing,

Iquitos in sprawl.

Don't answer. Don't answer. Don't answer.

African Night

A turban wrapping her head in silk,

White, full of moonlight

It falls, embracing her throat and shoulders

On its cascade in lavender to the floor.

Her hips, soft dunes

Glazed by shadows of trees that lie along its course

Become the path he will follow.

He won't return until morning.

Ethiopian Night

Ethiopian night,

Silent and filled with sound...

The sleigh-bells-jing of cricket's wings,

The lost mosquito invisibly acrobatic somewhere near,

A rooster's rustle at the end of his dream.

I am floating,

Inhaling the darkness.

Boundaryless, it flows in and out of my pores.

I can fly through the roof where once eucalyptus and

thatch might have captured me

Or the bougainvillea's thorns snared my hair.

Where a faint fragrance of incense and sheep

      pulses, then flees,

And the mud and straw that enclosed me

      have become only molecules bumping in the night.

And yet I did not disappear.

In the Ethiopian darkness, ancient devourer of men,

I bring you here

To lie beside me and listen to the owl,

To touch my fingers if the dawn should come.

Can you hear my heart beating?

Can you find me still?

I am here.

Ethiopia—The Road to Abra Minch

Streaks of yellow… one, two, three… flash by my window

As weaver birds race for first place atop the roof's thick

round thatch.

Squadrons are airborne,

Platoons rest amidst acacia thorns,

And a battalion of grackles walk in procession

Beside a hummingbird drinking deeply from a glowing

yellow iris.

As if sung from a Tower of Babel,

Accents of insects and birds flow through the air,

A squeaking, a popping, trills and clicks,

Rhythmic hoots, whirring and whines,

Polyphonic chants, that with a monk's ribbon of song to

the dusty rising sun,

Reminds the earth of its brotherhood.

Across the lake, Africa swells in striae of grey,

A gauzy aquarelle, where, as with the peoples here,

boundaries dissolve in time and histories

So old, that to remain unchanged seems the safest course.

And from behind the bougainvillea, a hidden child's voice

Weaves itself in contrapuntals and fugues

With the birds and the sheep and cattle and bees.

The voice swims with fish

And adorns the flowers that rise from cinnamon dirt.

Africa's children in eternal pregnancy from soil and sun—

May they prosper and grow across the land.

And if they falter, may they, like acacia arms,

Be born again...with shaking shoulders....

Strong and fierce and rising on a thermal wind.

Italian Summer

Grey sidewalks, viewed from above,

as my feet, like a tightrope-walker's, feel for crevices and

fractures, up-crops and odd, dimpled weatherings,

just right for cracking bones.

Beyond, in micro and often macro plastic waves,

Humanity surges into squared-piazzas,

Swelling against statues and chiseled granite walls,

A throbbing, electronic dead zone of wired-heads and

gelato-covered tongues that speak in many languages—

but only into phones.

Big hats, bulging busts and bellies, tennis shoes and saris,

black-African's muscled backs, chartreuse hair, flowered

gowns, bicycles and cars, shoulders pushing leather carts

of last year's "stuff" from China—

And the drums begin, the straight-legged dance of

Medieval retirees who pretend that glory is glimpsed again

on this swarming, faded postcard.

A Darkened Church in Florence

With big shoulders and puffed chest,

Flailing its baroque elbows sideways against each

buttressed flute,

The organ's surge pounds at Heaven,

Demanding—like a spoiled prodigy in a tantrum of

insufferability.

With bowed heads, those inside bend beneath each wave,

Elaborate fugues bringing them to their knees,

Holding them there

Until confessions pour forth in coins and tears.

A night in Florence,

A visit to God, or to effigies,

Who, with eyes turned skyward,

Break our hearts in the confines of a tiny church, on a tiny

street,

Where Heaven spills forth from copper lungs.

The Empress

I fly over Alps and Pyrenees,

Watching jagged purples advance their stab at Dolomites'

granite ribbons.

From my wooden bench in the churchyard's lee

Like a child or an ant or the honey bee insisting I am sweet,

I count the ranges and fill the gorges

With a kick of moss beneath my toe,

Blessing my domain with petals.

The Swallow's Moment

The shadows of ivy, blue along vanilla walls,

 its leaves like eyelashes spangled morning gold,

Tease softly in the air.

Two swallows in perfect tandem, swing out in horizontal

helix from stone arch to lichened tower.

This is their moment, in this ancient square, among these

restacked stories

That tumble like civilizations

As will these swallows, with but a few revolutions.

Sleep Well

Good night, sheep, that call with grandpa-voices and

discuss grass and shady sleeping-posts all day,

Good night, sheep, who "Ba" negatives and always walk in

single-file.

Good night, agreeing munchers, supporting every nay-say

that you hear.

Good night, sheep, who give weight to each day

 and pull wool to your chins when you sleep,

And salt the meadows with silver shadows

                    that Ba softly to me at night.

THE TIDES of LOVE

Lips

His Upper Lip

      It rises up as if from a fleshy undersea reserve,

      Swelling, developing, threatening to become

                  A claret-colored pillow

                    Beneath his nose.

His Lower Lip

      And below, a pitcher spout,

      Ceramic-turned and furled,

      A succulent and fulsome rose's petal,

                  Or a tumescent trumpet

                    Forming a song.

By His Own Hand

I didn't realize he had left.

I wasn't watching.

I didn't see him go.

And yet the world has changed.

The air has shifted,

The space that was his slowly filling with stardust.

And I miss him. This young man I didn't know,

Whose passing has moved the universe.

—

Our Brother's Keeper

I saw a mite greet a bee, carefully stepped and calm.

And nuzzling into her fur,

It climbed onto her back with the tenderest touch,

And settled in to kill her.

I saw a spore on a tree.

It flowered and grew, a spiraling ivory weapon.

It traced her with lace, and found its way in,

And gently proceeded to kill her.

I saw a man with no heart wrap his arms 'round a girl

And kiss her till her lips became his.

He entered her soul, seeding his will,

Animating his thoughts with her mind.

With no soul of his own, he'd found hers adrift,

A property ready for scavenge.

She was a beautiful host,

Now hollowed and dead,

—an empty tree in the forest.

The Good Mate

She sailed as she always had done, a good mate, anticipating each thought the captain had--asking curious questions about fuel consumption, width of beam, cost to pump out. She was the perfect boat guest. And a cook as well.

She could devise things only chefs yearned to do with bananas and rice or aging cans of corn. No matter the frozen milk, the rancid butter, the too littles and too muchs, the spoiled vegetables and the blackened fruit. She could turn it all into something good.

And even then, her skills didn't let up. Quickly cleaning dishes from each meal, she could wash them all in a coffee cup of suds, dry them well, bag the trash, wash the stove, and put the dishes into their sea-locked cupboards, never forgetting to sweep the galley and run the broom around the cockpit as well.

She quietly practiced knots in a corner and knew when a helmsman had strayed. Her courses were straight, she rarely luffed, and line-handling came like play.

Before bed, as she listened to other guests running down the water tanks, profligately taking ten-minute showers with the taps open wide, she took pride in her two cold cups per wash, the way she knew to run the shower sump till dry and never needed reminding to wipe down the tiny head's wooden walls.

Touching the mud of the Bay didn't faze her. Manning the pump-out of night-soil swirling through the vacuum's plastic tube only furthered the sense that she was competent, relied upon, and something like a sailor.

So why was it that late in the evening, the men put their arms around goofy women who only sun-bathed and did crossword puzzles? Why did they flirt with women who inanely screamed "woo-woo" whenever a drop of water hit them? Why did men reach out to steady healthy women with the natural balance of tightrope walkers, or refill their glasses just to hear them say, "Oh no, I really shouldn't."?

And so, the orange moon rolled across the sky and waving shadows of sea reeds nodded in the wind. At the stern, tipsy voices blended into dark humid air. And she sat at the bow watching an osprey soar, sequestered before the main, feeling—as she always had done, the familiar sense of competency.

To Sail the Sea

Don't pity the mariner who goes to the sea
With wife and loved ones calling him home,
Nor picture him fingering her photos and words,
Regretting the hours and days she will yearn.

For out on the ocean, Time fades away,
Its sameness weighting all moments as one.
The line of the sky, the circling clouds,
Invisible winds that embroider the sea
Settle the passions, flatten desire,
Reducing the soul to sensation.

Before is not here, After not born,
and consciousness rolls with the ocean.
A woman he knew waits somewhere for him,
and the man he was then still wants her.
But the ribbon of water, of days stitching Time
Has woven him into its fabric.

And he'll stay but a while, touching her face,
While hearing the sounds of the ocean.
Then soon he'll be gone, called to his home,
A dot drifting on the horizon.

The Moment Before

When time grows short,

When the valise stands

With its leather urgency near the door

Or beside the hand that will lift it

from its anonymity on the closet shelf to a weaponized

instrument of change,

I have noticed that lichen inches along the stones more

quickly,

That flowers advance their blooms.

I can hear silent swallow's considerations,

and watch as each droplet that falls from my pitcher

contains this reflected moment,

The round and crystalline hope

That you will not go

          on with the taxi's call.

That you will not bid me good-bye.

That in the end,

I will not leave you.

At the End

I didn't think it would end this way. Quiet as whispers in the night. The whirr of an air conditioner. And your voice coming sporadically, yet at last truthfully.

I didn't cry this time. Gutted again and again, the tears having long since drained away. Both of us, hollow people now, faintly remembering the dream we once might have dreamt together.

I remember—yet do not feel.

You feel only the residue of anger. Over and over you visit it. Piecing together the words. Inflections you recall that I did not utter. Accusations of intent where there had been only a desire to please. As if we spoke two languages; as if we acted in two plays.

Yet earlier this evening, you had called me "Sweetheart". And earlier still, "Baby." And before that, "My Sweetie-pie". Names that your lips form from habit, independent of your heart which has closed and long since left.

Once before you'd told me you no longer loved me. No, more—that you felt nothing when I entered a room. And nothing when I caressed you. And nothing when we would lie abed, the memories of our years together falling over us like autumn leaves on a harvested field.

And now, for the sake of kindness, you reach out and take my hand, and cover me in a blanket, and make me weep that you would at this last moment brush me with the gilt of love, but save its gold for someone who is yet to come.

For Sam in November

And just like that—

With the unanswered question,

The eye that held mine with sadness,

The bent head and vacant air

     that kept each of us from an embrace—

You became 'a man I used to know.'

You, cloaked in memories of anger and upset

     that rise around you like harpies,

     whispering as they devour love

     and leave their paranoid trail,

Me, remembering the happy love of your fingers in my

belt loop,

     The sighs of a man satiated by my flesh,

     The curl of your hair, the angled jaw,

     And a voice, that through the years,

     Wrapped me in a warm cocoon.

And now

You are to be 'a man I used to know'.

The clock, relentless beside me in the quiet of the night,

Pulses out the years that have fled,

> The smiles of children, the memory of houses,

> The memory of jobs, the lovers of my youth—

> Two men who married me

one who died and one who wished it—

Places and things and dear lovers I used to know.

But I didn't think it would be like that for us.

For us, old now, with our aches and wrinkles,

our funny set ways,

And our knowing—

Knowing what we have shown to the other,

What we didn't turn from seeing.

I thought we would be the lucky ones,

With a tender last love that would follow us to the end.

And instead, my dear,

With my picture in drawers and mementos bundled with twine,

I will soon become to you like the tick of the clock—

anonymous background,

A mental shadow,

Just a woman down the street

You used to know.

I Wonder About You (for Larry)

We were young that year.

Our skin was bronzed and sunlight splashed your hair,

And without really wanting to—I wondered about you.

We were grown-ups when you kissed my hands

And drew me a dream of a happy life,

And you were so sure, so sure,

That though I wondered about you—

I came along and lived with you the dream.

We were seasoned when the babies came

And grew and crept and cried,

And ran and fell and squealed with joy

And made us do the same.

And cookies, Scouts, and baseball,

Ballet and Wise Men in a play

Could never make you weary,

Never make you less than a river of love,

And my dear, believe me—I wondered about you.

And then like little ghosts, their laughter went away,

And quiet drifted down upon us,

Opaque and white and still,

Until, in the darkness of our sweet, warm bed,

I felt your safening presence and I wondered,

—maybe, it had always been about You.

Now, the evening comes in shadows,

Purple, blue and thick

And swallows up my watching at the window or the wood.

You no longer walk the path with me,

Nor waken from your dream,

And my thoughts cannot protect you from the journey that

you take.

But know, my love, that gently, when color streaks the sky

and robin voices rustle softly in the night,

That I draw you ever closer, like a warm and fragrant

cloak,

and watch a star's dark passing on its long

and wonderous voyage.

The Duke

The Duke, with starched white ruff,

satin sleeves and lacey cuff

Reclines against the damask,

a port held between his long pale fingers.

The shadows along his cheeks are geometric, allowing only

for the sequin-flash of softly hooded eyes,

Pools of darkness, luminous and moist,

While his bearded jaw, soft as the pelt of sable,

his manliness asserts.

Another hand, an arm extended, lies along his thigh.

His legs, open, powerfully at rest, capable of brutality,

stretch languidly toward me.

I wait in the twilight, watching as he turns toward the

softening scarlet of the night.

His eyes close as he remembers a passion lost, now

aroused by its memory.

In the stillness he sits thus alone,

     Not knowing

         that he has undressed me with his beauty.

For Doug

Do you hear the words between the oak tree's branches—

invisible ribbons sighing in the wind?

Listen, my love.

Listen among the shadows of our room.

In the warmth of the blanket that stretches across us like a

mother's arm.

Through the moist vapor of our breathing that rises and

falls... holds... waits for the other... and resumes

intertwined—you breathing what I have given you

and me, taking life from yours,

Listen.

And if a bird's murmured dream does not disturb you

nor moon-blue yet painted our walls,

You will hear the voices

      as they dance in poems above your head

            And wrap our nightly chrysalis in silver.

For Doug Again

The story we tell to each other day by day,

Like ants meeting along their journey,

A stop, a touch, a plan,

A direction to follow, one with the other,

A destination, a bound life—

This is the story I wish to hear.

Your whistle along a stony street,

Your hand reaching back to steady my way,

Gentle breathing after a chime of bells

That tells me you have wakened and

Are loving me softly in the night—

This is what I wish to know.

To tell our story with a face washed clean,

To hear our bodies croon,

Sculpting our tale in voices

That speak through rooms, across mountains, indelible—

This is the poem I write with you, my love,

Our curled letters become the lyrics of our life.

LOSS and METAMORPHOSIS

To Take A Chance

A broken egg, a stiff meringue,
 A yellow yolk for a cake,
An outcome unexpected,
For the chicken who took the time.

A pile of weeds at the sidewalk's edge,
Swollen hope of springtime gone,
Drying there for lack of form,
Unwanted 'chain migration.'

A pyramid of ants and dirt,
Historians and scholars,
Pheromone's tribal symmetry
Melted in my kettle's wash.

An egg, a weed, a scampering spec,
An issue of the Force that drifts
The pollen along my lash,
That crawls into my shoe,
That yearns to watch a chicken grow
And a child return from school.

Spots

I see them with an inner eye,
Molecules expanding into bugs and snowflakes,
And tiny grey eggs—unbroken for a Sunday omelette.

Stalker-like, I track them,
Picking one from the orange-peel host,
Vainly watching it dart and veer,
Vanishing near the horizon,
Only to appear, perversely, on a western rise.

Made of love, or just as elusive,
Galactic orbs dreamily float in the salt of tears,
My aquatic beginning—
Reminding me of its end.

Are they tiny messengers then?
Like the angels dying patients see
        in the week before they leave?
Swarming legions with warnings?
Or celestial bubbles meant to spirit me,
Giggling, into an existence
Where eyes are only for crying,
And a better view is had from within?

After the Accident

Alone in her body, in a room filled with the whispers of
machines that pump holy air deep into her chest,
Her breasts rise and fall unnaturally proud.
Her chin, held by a white plastic collar
that grips her like a malevolent hand,
gives her head a stubborn tilt.

She doesn't move much. Her arms are swathed in mittens
and canvas slings, suspending her, scarecrow-like, a limp
effigy, too weak to frighten birds, too frail to squeeze my
hand.
I watch the tube that reaches deep into her chest,
this blue and white pair of linear lungs
that give her skin the color of life.
I touch its plastic—my totem—
willing it to let the universe enter her and starlight
illuminate her weary spirit.

But she doesn't stir.
Far away, she seems to drift from moon to moon.
Her eyelids lift and fall again in conversation with the
planets.
And all the while blood flows and cells divide,
      and her pretty toes await their painting.

From a Maryland Hospital

"They've decided to do dialysis now."

   "Wanna get together later for pizza?"

"It's going to be a heart-lung bypass... tell mom."

   "You're so pretty, you could cause trouble."

"So, when he comes to, he'll probably be sent to jail..."

They spit out tendrils of their lives, like vines crawling into
cell phones, along corridors, in elevators and halls.

Draped in the sacred robes of this Temple of Woe,
acolytes march with bootied-feet
and shower-capped heads,
Sporting ecclesiastical scrubs in greens and pinks, or
preferentially, the pure white lab coat of an elder sage.

Of these priests and holy women no ethnic litmus-test is
required. Indians, Latins, Jews, and Blacks—but if you're
really lucky, a tiny-eyed, fast-walking Asian will pass
mysterious fingers across your brow, and amidst
incantations and ancient signs... 'Albumin reduced at 66;
OPS is 2; LBG's on 16; Hgb 27'... you will feel the malady
flee and the breath of life return.

High above the cafeteria sounds and the testimonials as to
why Jeremy is a jerk or Publix has better bread,
And far from an intern's ambition and a drug rep's much-
awaited bonus... lies my daughter.

At 33, broken into pieces and her life's blood nearly all left
in a pool by the highway's edge.

Oh God, that one day she will once more hold a cell phone
and argue and giggle and take the long way home through
the woods,
And make spinach pies and smoke too much and hold the
hand of her son.
Until then, please let her have an Asian priest,
and machines with good batteries,
and bags dripping elixirs filled with years of life,
And magic mantras that circle her body and recommend
her to a white-coated god.

Four Poems from an Emergency Room

Simpering cadence that bleats its way along his wrist,

A yes, a no, and a dash to the finish.

His heart thumps merengues, tangos and the sway of palms,

And he lies there, still as a dance floor,

waiting for the next act.

Her silhouette, black as a fist, sits before the window,

An aura of hair making her a spinning planet,

An old and tiny orb, soon to be free in the Cosmos.

There is a white-rimmed beach at the base of an undulating hill,

And in little inward tiers, the hue deepens to liquid

Like an oddly red pond, frozen, perhaps, and slick.

He looks into his wound—and he goes sailing.

In the waiting room girlfriends giggle and old men ogle and

children strain their necks toward TV.

A cyclist's spandex spotlights his bum, women's lips are

repainted.

But someplace near, inhaling air gone stale,

a number behind a curtained wall,

Her fingers move, the talking shadows traced,

Feeling for a life that cracked and fell, like a porcelain cup

from which the tasty juice has dried.

With Doug in May

In a room whose colors are meant to deceive,
To disappear into platitudes, positionless, formless,
Not leading you on,
I wait for a man.

It's cold in here.
Linoleum and plastic, stainless steel and grey curled cords
That eye my ankle like snakes
Seem disinterested in the form beneath the blanket.
The man, swathed in tubes, basketed behind railings,
in this room of empty hums,
Is already theirs—
To feed, to squeeze,
to sip from like birds from his very veins.

The gauges aren't measuring what we breathe here.
The in-and-out, the pulse of fear... and more,
The not-understood, the not-spoken,
The circles of guesses that like a children's game of toss,
Pile up and tell us that secrets far worse
lie in muscles and nerves,
Or amorphous caches that will change our lives.

Yet we remain solitary prisoners of this place,
willing participants in our prosecution.
In-between—
In the white detention center before the jury is called,
Before the door opens.
Before we are warm again

The Hurricane

The cat's head peeks from behind a chair,

Retreats,

Then turns toward the window, draped by the coming

storm as if in mourning.

Waiting—we glance at each other and at the room

Whose contents, normally non-descript,

Have taken on a meaning. A potential.

The trajectory of our demise

should the storm invite itself inside.

A sofa, a straight-backed chair, the crystal lamp,

My cat and me.

Like patients awaiting their surgeon,

Or the sleeper, the third noise in the night.

We sit in the darkened room, count seconds before the

next flash,

And presume to think ourselves permanent.

When even the cat knows he's not supposed to fly.

The Day That Peter Died

A simple walk,
A brilliant day,
The sun wrapping and unwrapping itself around the trunks
of trees and slithering along the grass.

A breeze strikes up a dance, a tango that gathers leaves
like willing maidens, pivoting them, flashing their golden
faces and ruddy skin this way and that,
each a teasing coquette—each at their final ball.

But without farewell,
With no hesitation nor reciprocal grasp,
One leaf, spotted and worn,
 releases its hold and sets itself free.

Through layers of space in helixed descent,
The leaf seems not interested in the party above
 where 'dancers' entwine and careen
in pas de deux and pas de quatres.

In its solitary waltz, exposed and translucent, an expelled
debutante or a rebellious teen, it swirls in scalloped arcs,
reaching upward, tilting down,
Until, at last, in exhalation,
its golden points recline into the dirt.

On this brilliant day,
At this unique moment,
The sun gilding a sky of dancing shadows against a canopy
of Wedgewood blue,
Life ends.

Once part of a whole with veins and substance
A leafy life lived in a community of peers,
It crumbles now, umber at my feet, scratching its
silhouette against the soil.

I stop, facing the leaf, to wonder at its singularity.
The curled tips, desiccated bronze; the scars; the parasitic
mounds it has fought off in life, and which in death, adorn
it like encrusted gems.

Yet here is a death unmourned,
In the quiet of an autumn morning when nobody looked
and nobody cared.
A leaf was all— a spasm of life, a thrust toward the sun.

From this corporeal tree,
From this place in the park,
From this city, this country, this tiny ball of blue,
One unique leaf among a million others,

One I will miss for the rest of my life.

The Daring Spider

How foolish the squirrel on the feeder's roof, a target for a
hawk's midday meal.
And unwise the golfers, in their oranges and reds, signaling
the sniper to squeeze.
How daring the spider, who leg over leg, fondles his web
into shimmers,
while a cardinal nearby follows each move—
the assassin bent on assignment.

The old woman taps on the walk with her cane,
its fissures seductive entrapments,
as she shuffles among them, oblivious victim to the
obviously victimless crime.
While an unthinking mother and her vulnerable child
expose their pale flesh to a crowd of waddling ducks at the
side of a lake with a choice of death by drowning—
(Or a more prosaic end by a peck.)

Cautionless players, tempting the killers, the shooters and
those packing poison,
The bombers, the beaters, the oblivious drivers, the rapists
with their rapiers drawn,

To walk down a street, faces exposed, or to laugh in a
crowd to be shot,
To tremble your leaf, or step from your nest,
to walk alone 'neath the moon,
Is a gamble for living, a hand raised for breathing
(though both will ultimately kill you.)

It is a swim in the nude with rocks nearby,
A dance with a stranger on New Year's,
Conceiving a child who will make you cry,
Knowing suicide is just over-rated.

So, I will go to the mosque, the temple, the club,
I'll do yoga and go to my high school.
I will dance in the street and see films in the dark—

And I'll wiggle my web 'till it shimmers.

The Goose's Walk

In this beautiful park on a cerulean day, a goose walked by
me toward the road.
Wise and purposeful,
she launched each foot before her.

An iconic goose, the prototypical goose, made to see and
admire.
I watched her undulating neck with its stationery head,
how the sun turned her black wings blue,
How as she stepped toward the roadway's shade, the car
so quickly splayed
apart her breast and torqued her throat in its dying coil.
And its swiftness left me breathless.

The edge of change.
The man with the knife before he will murder.
The loving wife in the moment before hearing of the affair.
The passenger in the terminal whose flight will never land.
The aerialist who knows for one elongated second that
things have come—unbalanced.

The edge of things.
The Before and The After.
Unknowing—then changed.
The sight before blindness —and perhaps worse, its
reverse.

I saw Jesus beaten to death in a church yesterday. The actors knew he would die, but I wished he had fought back. I wish the aerialist would have parachuted; the passenger switched to a train. I wish for the wife a prosperous divorce and the goose a benign flutter on the windshield of the car.

But the edges, like faults, like crevasses opening beneath our feet keep coming. The moment before and the always after. Unseen abysses, bad news, shocking knowledge, mental tattoos in indigo ink that once were unwritten.

And so—with the goose—marching forward into life's traffic, too late for anticipation,
teetering on the cusp of an outcome unknown,
I look toward the trees,
     And sense that like me,

        the leaf does not believe it will fall.

A PLACE of SOLACE

PUYCELSI, FRANCE

Puycelsi 1

It's as if each time you arrive in Europe,
eager for the person you will be at the
end of the voyage,
You must, like a fetus on its way to birth, cycling through
each stage of primordial development first,
Begin your journey where you were before,
Helpless, "gill-breathing", a reptilian vestige seeking light,
Seeking enlightenment in the developed eye,
the human sensibility,
All the things left here before in that earlier Darwinian
struggle.
All the things lost with the return to ooze—

                             the flight to Omaha—

The salamander-life renewed.

Puycelsi 2

A photo of a stone,

Ice cream-trickles along a chin,

A spin to the altar to stir the musty air,

The forced murmur of interest in a nameless saint and

Heads that bob from ancient house to gardens untended

—those green Edens of twisted trunks,

those Renaissance twiglets grown old.

The tourists pay an hour's homage

To a dream they'd all once had.

But now, like a trip to the grocer's and a perusal of his
wares,

They choose a plump green vista (fresh enough to last the
flight)

And leave the rest on the village shelf.

Thank god, thank god, thank god.

Puycelsi 3

Does God really notice
that his gilded angels are covered in dust?
That his mother was carved as a dwarf?
That the high hopes and skipped meals of peasants hoping
for a back-slap in paradise,
Who hocked the farm for centimes to make this church a
heaven-way-from-heaven,
Would now, for Him, be shrug-bait—
His disappointment showing at the buckled plaster and
empty pews—
      And not one candle to make Him feel good?

Yet in this cold and hollow room,
Vaulted, arched, and smelling of a crypt,
There is solace of a kind.
A pigeon-choir sermonizes just outside the door,
Feathers falling in the heat,
While in this coolness, this flaking mausoleum,
I let my mind wander to God
And nap along with the fly at my side,
Receiving a nonchalant blessing,
      From both my Maker and the fly.

Puycelsi 4

Lacey silhouettes, sky-tatted by hungry bombardiers,

their little phalanxes disappearing with each post-prandial

bug—

The morning sky lingers, pewter-blue,

loathe to give way to the on-coming hour

when the creamy smell of sheep

and the grass they will chew comes heavy with the sun.

I see the rocky cliff where ancient bison fled, leaping for

their lives with only bones left for sifting,

And heretical tracks, where Cathars fled as well,

Their hopes now mere museum geology.

Then I cut my peach, and eat my bread, dust bees from

inside my flower,

And walk the cliffs and leafy paths,

and slumber in the soil.

Puycelsi 5

I sit on the cool stone steps, a petrified spiral behind me,

To contemplate the afternoon.

The hours pass, while the day remains,

One hour tossed to fingernails' curve, another for a wasp's

survival,

More to voices near my shutters

As understood as the pigeon kerfuffle that clucks delight in

the eves.

On this drowsy noon, when a hot mistral shenanigans

across fields of flowers,

Their upturned faces and yellow smiles, each in obedient

swivel,

I stare at the oak of a hand-turned leg, lost in its

labyrinthine grains,

then notice the man in the room with me,

Another piece of quiet wood.

Puycelsi 6

The shadows of ivy, blue along vanilla walls,

its leaves like eyelashes spangled morning gold,

Tease softly in the air.

Two swallows in perfect tandem, swing out in horizontal

helix from stone arch to lichened tower.

This is their moment, in this ancient square, among these

restacked stories

That tumble like civilizations.

As will these swallows, with but a few revolutions.

Puycelsi 7

The ivy grows sideways here, circling the stones in green
waves,
Last year's naked remnants leaving dark intaglios—the
route to follow.
The churchyard would be quiet,
solitude on a rounded bench beneath a tree,
but the grandmotherly pigeons are thinking out loud,
cursing into their breasts as they waddle along a cornice,
deriding the swallows' acrobatic feats.

Puycelsi 8

How long does the magic last in the new place?
With the new house?
With new apples to pick, new wine to taste,
A tactical reframing before the surprised gasp and the
novel charm remind you of the day before
When you were even then less astonished?

In this tiny village, suspended among chattering birds,
floating across ochred wheat and a Roman forest so thick
the bees must wait outside,
I touch the stones from childhood,
And childhoods not my own.
I remember thoughts I'd left here, buried near the well.
And I speak a language understood by sheep who tell me
not to leave.

To be an outsider, with nothing here to bind, but the
beauty in the lichen and the season's fragrant turns,
Then feel time shift with a medieval brush of a sleeve I felt
when dreaming,
Is to posit that the ghosts still want me here
to keep their magic potions,
To feed them wonder every day
 and then return the favor.

Puycelsi 9

In my kitchen, the fly paper curls like amber,
A sticky, glistening come-on, a cautionary for baby bugs.
And by the sink, a breeze twice-boiled, lifts the curtain's
lace,
A hide and seek with the stony wall, it rifts along the
tatting—
Arpeggios of air like bridal veils when discretion's no
longer needed.

The wood, the wind, the hollyhocks that summer here
then dance away for winter,
The candlesticks and smell of grass,
Late wines of last September,
The half-grown lambs and muttering dams, whispering
secrets to the trees,
And now this honey bee, who sweetly stings,
Remind me of the fickle spring
                              and seasons that must not be trusted.

Puycelsi 10

Which is to be dreaded most?

The isolation of a cell in which the years will watch you dying?

The fiction of a marriage with electronic barricades?

The sailors' plight, with sweltering afternoons when the wind grows stale and there is no course to home?

Or the ancient village in summer heat, its stones a pyre, and not a vacation?

The days of each, precious days, pages unwritten, dreams already spent at wakening,

Cloudy horizon-shapes that refuse animation,
That come and go, like footsteps on a rocky path.

But they are not your footsteps.

They are not your shoes.

The reluctant trod is not made by you.

Puycelsi 11

A little gargoyle's mouth is open wide, spitting impolitely
the rain we've waited for for days.

Days so hot that no one thinks, patting their red, swollen
faces and shrugging a French, "What can you do?"

But now, each valley in the lichened tiles is filled with tiny
effluviums,

Dimpled with rain drops as cold as ice, baby Niagaras for
bees.

And now, we think, a thought might survive,
Some insight at last will be found.

Yet I'm not sure I want the revelation,
the mystic vision glimpsed by my inner eye.

But rather to listen
To the water splash on hand-hewn rock and the
hollyhock's dainty dress,

To the way the church bell speaks its patient invocation
through the rain.

Puycelsi 12

Instead of wires, black bindings of electrical efficiency
running across the sky,

I see birds scalloping the air, silent ballerinas breakfasting
in the breeze.

Instead of horns, honking exasperation, I hear a soft bell
from a bullock's neck—
and his cows' answer in agreement,

And an ivory necklace of obedient sheep calling
encouragement as they 'Ba' their way to morning grass.

Instead of skyscrapers, erupting manfully from the earth,
Challenging the very space they occupy,

I see the skin of the planet, like a pelt, tanned here from
the sun, lush there with new growth,

A spackle of creation, of substance and scent, a dozen
greens, ochres and blues,

A salmon sunset, hours out of memory,
And the new day's lifting of this starry veil.

Puycelsi 13

I would come here in winter when the old men and the ghosts are about,

When the ivy recedes to tracery, black intaglios of summer.

I would hear the birds' complaints at a slinking cat whose faithless owner forgot its charm,

And I would count the bee's hours, ignoring the bells' command to prayer,

Nestling beneath covers, with croissant dreams for comfort.

Marina Brown is author of two award-winning novels.

Land Without Mirrors and *Lisbeth* each won Gold Medals for Literary Fiction from the Florida Authors and Publishers Association and *Lisbeth* won a Silver Medal in the Royal Palm Literary Competition. Her short stories and poetry have also won awards.

Brown's other books include *Walking Alone Together*, 12 stories at the end of life, and *Airport Sketches, a Week of Lives at the Tallahassee Airport*. She is a correspondent with the Tallahassee Democrat and writes for Florida Design Magazine, Tallahassee Magazine, and Vires Magazine.

Brown's other interests include painting, with one-man shows at Meek-Eaton Black Archives, the Tallahassee Airport Gallery and the Gadsden Art Museum, as well as dancing, playing the cello, sailing, and speaking French and Italian... and always, always traveling.

February, 2019

54966047R00069

Made in the USA
Columbia, SC
08 April 2019